MW01094822

dear human

dear human

Kay Eck

genuine press

Dear Human
Copyright © 2021 by Kay Eck

Printed in the United States of America

Genuine Press
Sawyer, MI
www.kayeck.com

LCCN: 2021909319
ISBN: 978-1-7365831-2-8

For the women who loved me
while I was learning to love myself.

Christine Denz
Donna Miceli
Lisa Bodett
and
Mary Lou Quirk

ALSO BY KAY ECK

Divorce: a love story

The author's moving and melodic memoir of her map-less journey to consciously uncouple from her husband of nearly 30 years.

Alive & Kicking: stories of waking up

Podcast featuring people from all walks of life, each on a unique human journey toward spiritual awakening. Find these inspiring stories at www.kayeck.com/podcast.

All poetry within is the work of the author and may be credited as such.

CONTENTS

Tell me not of your feats and goals
Or even your hopes and joys
I want to hear about the mistakes you've
made

Tell me about the knots in your trapezii
What knots your belly
The things too heavy to set down just yet

I want to live in a world where my
outstretched hands
Become the place you drop your riven
bits of humanness
And know that mine will land in yours

Introduction

Your life is a love letter penned by the Author of All Things.

Everything about you is a unique sentence that when scrawled across the sky of existence forms a paragraph, a page, and then a story. A love story—a tale no one else can tell. But the intended audience for this letter is not another reader nor the critic. It is only for you. You are both the protagonist and the one for whom the myth has been written, and it could be titled, *The Truth of You.*

Your life unfolds like the turning of a page, and with every word you may glimpse a little deeper into the world of you. Your life tells you who you are, why you are here, where you have been, and where you are going. Every evolving moment, from the seemingly insignificant to the profound, is an opportunity to know, accept, and love yourself more deeply. And while it has all been masterfully designed to reveal you to you, clarity can be hard to come by when you are in the thick of it, making your way through the minefield of being a person on the planet at this time. Through this sweet and sloppy mess.

Some people seem to catch on to the plot quite naturally. Their curiosity and senses sharpen at the first whiff of smoke in their lives. They immediately burrow about for the meaning under the circumstances. For others, the house must be in flames, hooks and ladders must be onsite, and people in protective gear must be shouldering through the front door before they awaken to what their lives want to teach them.

For most of us, it is probably something in between, like:

> a persistent dissatisfaction, a something's missing type of thing
>
> a heartache that doesn't want to heal
>
> a growing disillusionment with the status quo
>
> a bit of a knot in the stomach or some inexplicably sweaty palms
>
> a subtle sadness or quickness to tears

We may overlook or avoid these things not because we are stubborn or slow but because something in us knows that if we open that bottle just a bit, the genie will indeed jump out. It likely will be big, maybe bad, and there will be no chance of stuffing it back in. But, what if this one act of getting curious about your human condition is the first step toward a life of true joy, real peace, and lasting love? Could you welcome that kind of transcendence through trial?

There is no getting around the fact that awakening to your true self can sometimes feel like part or the whole of your life is unraveling. In a way, that is true. It is as if the crude veneer is cracking off and falling away so that you can see the radiant work of art underneath. This can be a demanding, disorienting, and humbling process if all you have ever known is the veneer. But it is worth it.

We came to experience humanity's astounding complexity. It is painful, grace-filled, and everything in between. As a collective, we are growing more aware every day. This group wisdom supports us individually to master the process with more ease and empowerment. Once we understand how our lives are supporting us—adoring us even—the things we may have thought we couldn't bear become more manageable. Healing happens. As we gain dexterity, everything starts to feel like a gift, and we become more masterful at the art of living.

We are born seekers set in forward motion, each blazing our own trail. We are intrepid explorers with the necessary spunk and stamina to walk this path. If you let it, your life will lead you through the labyrinth of lessons that simultaneously still the feverish mind and excite the inner spark creating the conditions that allow you to see the magnificent, invincible truth of who you are.

No matter what you are encountering or how clumsily you may be piloting through it, your life is a love letter, written by the universe, loving you unconditionally. It has been crafted with the greatest appreciation for your courage, strength, and willingness to love your life as it is loving you. Once you know this, you won't want to spend another minute without its words upon your being, immersing yourself in the mystery and depth of your gorgeous life like a letter you can't wait to tear open.

Someone recently asked what qualifies me to write a book like *Dear Human*. I don't think he meant to ask about credentials such as degrees and job experience, which is fortunate because I don't have any. I think he wanted to know what I had suffered and survived. What could I say other than that I have suffered and survived all of life up until now. Isn't this true for us all? The question is, are we willing to *thrive*?

The path of consciousness, to me, is becoming aware that nothing highlights transcendence quite like trial. Though we are no longer restricted to just this paradigm, ultimately we each have chosen the human experience for its capacity to show us both contrast and all-encompassing beauty. If I have any qualification it is that after much avoidance and countless missteps, I have fully embraced this rather challenging setup. That, and there is no sense denying it, I have begun to thrive!

I was born with a longing to serve and the curious ability to love the essential innocence of humanity, no matter what it gets up to. It has taken me awhile to figure out that the execution of that service is just to be myself and to let you be yourself. It sounds so simple and sweet, like second grade. But it can be so, so hard.

I wrote *Dear Human* because I want you to know the exhilarating freedom of your power to reveal the exquisite truth and beauty of your life and to feel the love and support that are always with you. If you are reading this now, perhaps you have sent up a little beacon. My prayer is that *Dear Human* will help.

Even if we are not yet acquainted, I know we are on to something wonderful together. I could not—and would not—want to do it without you. We are kinfolk, lost and found, in the process of growing toward one another. I am as grateful for your life as I am for my own, for they are one and the same, with many captivating expressions.

We have been on this great journey together throughout all of life. And together we go, burrowing about for the meaning of it all. May your ears, mind, and heart be filled with the compelling poetry of your boundless life.

—k.e.

I sat down to record my conclusions
But received only queries.
Is there only one question
With eight billion answers
Or eight billion questions
With just one answer?

Dear Human,
Wade into the river of love.

Through all of life runs a river of love that has kept us flowing in trust with the current. The river of love is the only thing that is real; the challenges we face are just scenery along the way.

The longer we are on the river, the more expert we become at paddling, more skilled at shifting our view from the distracting scenes playing on the banks and back to the river itself. We begin to understand that our craft is water-worthy and built to last. We come to see that the river of love does not have a destination, and it does not anticipate obstructions ahead. Its nature is not to know but to remain in flow.

Our ways of being in relationship with life do not change the river's route or its ability to hold us afloat. Whether bobbing at the surface or when submerged, there is no separation between us and the river. It runs through us and around us, under and above us. Whatever we have been, whatever we become, it is because of the river of love. It runs forever, circling back to its headwaters, creating a loop of love that never ends.

All we ever need to know is that we are in its flow.

Dear Human,
Heed the call to dwell deeply.

Our hearts are calling like a dinner bell at dusk, asking us to come see what has been prepared. The heart is our call to dwell deeply in life.

Like a compass, the heart is a dependable guide for finding beauty, peace, connection, and renewal. As a power station with a direct channel to divine truth, it cannot be externally influenced or corrupted. The heart is infallible, trustworthy, and pure. And while it has the potential to lead you to a life of radiant purpose, it does not do so without your invitation. To play with the heart's miraculous gifts, you have to be in a conscious relationship with it. You must look into its eyes, tell it what you need, and listen when it speaks.

To say the least, we are not accustomed to doing this.

Modern society teaches that the intellect is king. Our education system fills our minds with facts, figures, and formulas, and it does nothing to develop our connection to the heart. As we have become overly reliant on our noisy minds to manage our reality, the voice of the heart recedes. But the mind is only as good as the information it is fed. The mind alone cannot and is not meant to know what is true or to make choices for us. Intuition, guidance, and discernment are the heart's terrain.

I spent decades trying to achieve success with my mind at the helm even though this was not my nature. As a child, I was curious, creative, and tenacious. I loved to test my body and my courage. In the quiet moments, I felt connected to the heavenly realms and genuinely cared for those who didn't seem to believe they were cared for. But it was not hard to see that none of that was particularly valued in school, so I began to believe I was rather unexceptional and to conclude that a developed mind was the worthiest achievement.

This belief prevailed through my college days and early career. I was somewhat successful, but I was not happy. The unexpected blessing of motherhood was that it allowed me to release at least some of my ideas about success in the world. I let myself be fed by love and reenter the world of play—to remember who I was and what brought me joy.

Since then, the more intimate my relationship with my heart's true nature has become, the more successful I feel. Of course, my definition of success has evolved as well. Now it is defined by depth, meaning, purpose, and service with the accompanying benefits of contentment, connection, gratitude, and joy.

Your genius—that which makes you truly extraordinary—is not about what is in your mind. It is about what is in your heart. Even the most brilliant people long mostly to love and be loved. When you wield the power of the heart in your own life, you can do astonishing things. But what is remarkable is that when your life is lived in service to your heart, everything you do is astonishing. Seemingly small things infused with great love tether the world to its evolutionary journey. There, in the heart-sphere, everything makes sense.

You matter. You always have, and you always will.

You are here with a unique purpose—to reveal your life's divine potential and what virtuosities are yours alone. The spirit you infuse into the prismatic mix will never fade. The way you live life stretches the confines of how life can be lived. What you learn expands the vocabulary of what can be known. Indeed, your contribution is the missing link that makes everything complete. Long after you have gone, the universe will go on heralding your great and meaningful presence.

This is how much you matter.

In the disarray of everyday life, however, it is hard to see that any one person matters. You may lose track of your life's point or get so tangled up in obligations to others that you misplace its meaning. We have been deeply conditioned to believe that it is wrong to dedicate ourselves to our own happiness. And we have been taught that tending to the needs and desires of others is the kindest way to be in the world. This has had disastrous effects on us individually and collectively because not mattering to yourself is like a misaligned cog that causes the whole machine to malfunction.

Mattering to yourself is not selfishness. It is a responsibility. When you place yourself highest on the list of things that need attention, you create a cared-for you with a cared-for life that is healthy and whole and highly functioning. When you matter to yourself, you become so deeply nourished by paying attention to your own needs that you are no longer depleted. There is ample time to fulfill all your dreams, tend to the essential demands of life, and also to serve others, freely, without obligation.

When you matter to yourself, it becomes impossible to deny others this freedom. When no one is wearing themselves thin with forced obligation, each can devote their energy to what brings the greatest joy and effect, to reach for their God-given potential. Everyone expands their capacity to bring their gifts to the whole. And together, each in harmony with their inner purpose, the machine begins to make magic.

When I launched what I am now calling my *I Matter* campaign, I had to start small and practice. It was not a grand, sweeping movement that came all at once. The mere utterance, *I Matter*, was all I had, but it was enough of a beginning. The campaign gained strength as I stayed home rather than attend a meeting that would surely tax my strength and eat up my hours. Or, when I shut the door and turned on the bath or sat on the porch observing life instead of filling it with more chores.

I paid attention to the voice within that was chiding me for being selfish. I noticed that the litany of demands came not from others but from somewhere inside of me. *You should be doing this. You should be doing that.* I realized that whomever those voices once belonged to, I had made them mine. So I could just as easily change the narrative to one that celebrated my willingness to matter to myself.

I started to assess how often I did something for which the only motivation was joy or delight or simply because I wanted to, and how many times I did something out of obligation. And what outcome was created by these very different states of doing. I considered the whole of the list, checking to see how out of balance I was—too much acting from obligation and not enough out of mattering to myself. Bringing my life into better balance gave me the endurance to face bigger issues such as why I was placing my dreams on the back burner while prioritizing everyone else's. And why I was unable to voice my desires and beliefs in important relationships.

Ultimately, I learned that, as hard as they might try, no one can convince you that you matter. That is not a gift another can give. You must give it to yourself. You must decide that you matter.

There is a silver thread connecting you with life itself, and the insistent tug you feel, drawing you nearer, is courage. Your life beckons like a secret lover, and even though you may taste the metallic risk in your mouth, you must move toward it. Though it might be easier to ignore the call, it is somehow more painful as well. Living life halfway is also half-dying. Why not live life fully so that you may leave whole?

Instinctively, you already know that living life requires the totality of being human—that despite your outer circumstances, you will experience everything there is to experience on the inner plane. This is the irrevocable pact you made with life in your birthing.

Our experiences and characteristics are not the same. Some people seem to have lives that require an almost obscene amount of courage, and some seem to have been granted a clear patch of ice. But none of us really avoids skating with the vital questions or grappling with our predicaments. That, we share.

When you have no choice but to walk, courage is what arises between your step into the unknown and the moment your foot lands on the pavement a million miles away. It is not something you can access or even count on until you are well into the need for it. You cannot summon courage. It summons you.

But life also is in covenant with you. There were promises made, and those promises have been kept. On the other side of ungodly challenge are the things you most desire, and everything you require to get there is within you.

The bravest act, bar none, is to try to love. It means taking your:

> *Please don't hurt me*, and
> *I'm not sure about you*, and
> *I'm not sure about me*, and
> *This could end badly*, and
> *I have trouble trusting*, and
> *I'm feeling lonely*, and
> *I wonder if I am enough*, and
> *Is love even possible*, and

Putting them behind your

I'm willing to try.

Our intrepid willingness is the key that unlocks all doors. No matter how we feel we may have failed or fallen short in the past, when we marry our hearts to our prayers we send them out into the world in the hopes of loving and being loved despite everything.

Dear Human,
Life will ask things of you.

Life puts us on a high wire and asks us to dance a tango with surrender as our partner.

What we may learn is that artful falling is not a failing, nor a quitting. It is living with the knowledge that we know nothing and, so, must trust completely.

To flail or to fly makes no difference. With our arms flung wide in a state of faith, we fall into and out of everything. We tumble to the Earth upon our birth. We spill from childhood into adolescence, adulthood into old age. We fall in and out of love. We dip in and out of shadow.

In this, a falling place, we are never alone, and we have already prepared our own safe landings. What awaits at the bottom of our freefall is more life. And more love.

I fell to the Earth with a thud,
Let the fen soak my back
And moss approach.
I let the dense air there
Squeeze certain things into me and
Other things out of me.
I watched all manner of weather pattern
Carve a topography out of me.
I lay still, seemingly dead
Until the insistent sun drew sweat.
Things grew, trees and weeds,
And over time I became a thicket,
Stalwart and silent 'round the edges,
Tangled and teeming within.

As a child, faith came easily to me. I did not doubt my place in the spirited essence of everything around me. I had a clear sense of my goodness and the goodness in others. I somehow trusted that to run down grassy hills, lie on the hot sand, and hold my mother's hand were consecrated privileges. What came to eclipse that was a complex and punitive system of rules, exclusions, and layers of human interference.

As the years rolled by, I began to sense that the more compliant I became, the more lifeless I felt. The more ardently I worked to match the standards set for me, the less innocent I knew myself to be. The more power I ceded, the smaller I became. My religious experience was slowly draining the spirit right out of my soul. Lost, angry, and without any clarity about what I was doing, I took a hard left and let go of what little faith remained.

I spent years wandering around like a lost lamb, engaging in the self-defeat of bad decisions, unworthy people, and wrong roads. I felt bonded to something beyond myself in this world, but I had little faith in it. I tried different approaches to the world of spirit, but nothing seemed to fit. I sought therapy, which helped with some things, but not everything.

At times I was terrified, as though I were riding a bicycle on a fence rail, awaiting the inevitable crash. Mostly, I felt defeated by disappointment and exhausted by fear of judgment. My dimmer switch seemed to be set to functional, subtle sorrow.

Despite all this, I found real love with a good person. Then, one at a time, just as each drop of honey makes the tea a bit sweeter, my children renewed my faith in the purity and innocence of humanity. But looking into their faces each day only solidified my understanding of how little esteem religion had for it.

In hindsight, I can see that what was occurring within me was an epic recalibration. Like a giant wheel was grinding to a halt and starting the slow, almost painful work of rotating in the opposite direction. In giving up on ideas of an external source of sacredness, I was allowing for the nurturance of the sacred within me. In rejecting the authority of others over me, I was beginning the hard task of establishing jurisdiction over my mind, body, heart, and soul.

This was the gift of my disbelief.

I came to see that, for me, disbelief is intrinsic to belief in the same way that sadness is intrinsic to happiness. If something in me did not believe, I would not be in a state of disbelief. This is no different than when you are sad, it is because you know that happiness exists. There is a tension between belief and disbelief. But really, they are opposite sides of the same coin. They are both aspects of faith.

I no longer need to be reminded of my place in the complex web of all things even as it increasingly defies description. Now, my faith is to remain in prayer with purposeful wondering about all I cannot yet know. It is my trust that everything I experience on the Earth plane is an exercise in seeing through the eyes of the Divine, a nonstop business of trying to wipe the grime off my lenses. It is, I have found, enough work for a lifetime.

Twin flames of belief and disbelief

Rival aspects of the same longing

Have me inching up the ladder

Relentlessly reaching

Somewhere for something

They love and bicker

Flexing foreign muscles and

Up I go

They kiss and slash

Dance and throw stones

Then rest on even rungs

And up I go

Dizzy and fast past my comfort zone

Sick and thrilled from ascending tension

You are a heroic human being set upon a path of accelerated learning and growth. This sometimes feels like a steeplechase course for advanced equestrians in which you are riding on the back of a bucking bronco. Please take a moment to give yourself a high-five just for showing up each day. Yes, here, there will be participation medals.

As you begin to truly honor yourself in this life, which you so deserve, you will come to love both your action and inaction, your purpose and pointlessness, your achievement and your nothingness, your triumphs and your setbacks. You will love all of the energy that is required to do everything and to do nothing and all of the feelings you have about your experiences. This does not happen all at once, moments before the awards are announced. It is a process of revealing and rejecting all the tricky ways you have of not honoring yourself.

We were trained early to seek external rewards, and it grows from there. Treats, grades, degrees, certificates, promotions—we happily accept every recognition without realizing they are ways in which we let other people determine our value. And if we are good at that game, we become eligible for the visible rewards of success such as hot spouses, hip kids, great trips, and fancy homes. The underlying sentiment is that our purpose here on the planet is to accomplish things—here's your life, do something with it. The bigger the better.

Even within the spiritual community, success is sometimes measured by progress toward a goal. It is almost mandated that we manifest our worldly desires and create our best lives. We sometimes forget that these outcomes are not the goal. Spirituality is the self exploring its unlimited *internal* nature. The rewards of that—peace, clarity, spaciousness, compassion, and self-love—are invisible to the naked eye. The good projects, clients, networks, or abundance that may or may not follow are not the point.

Playing at this does not make us bad people. It just means that we have been set within a system in which our true value has been masked, and our challenge is to wade through it to find what is truly worthy of our honor.

Despite what society tells you about finding your purpose, your purpose is set by you, may be known only to you, and can change throughout your life as determined by you. Because it is your purpose for your life, nothing outside of you has any bearing on whether it has value or not. It does not have to be grand. What better purpose might there be than to tend a little garden, make a nice coffee cake for friends, live to feel the sun on your face, or make a child, animal, or plant feel preposterously wanted?

This is not to say that setting goals and achieving things or owning stuff are empty pursuits. But honor yourself by doing it only for your own enjoyment, growth, and challenge and not in exchange for the favor of others.

When you can honor all of you and all of your experiences, you cannot be diminished in any way. If you hold yourself in the highest esteem, no individual, committee, or institution can legitimately weigh in on your value. You cannot be controlled by external compensations that keep you in a low-grade state of underwhelming satisfaction, anxiously and continuously striving for more.

Let *you* be the most powerful and influential person in your life. Choose to be revered by the only one who truly matters, and let no one else get a vote.

I do not find myself to be lovable all the time. I definitely don't find others and the world at large to be consistently lovable. I am trying to get there, but I often fall short. When unconditional love is not achievable for me, I reach for compassion.

Compassion is the almost illogical ability to extricate yourself from some troubling thing and to view yourself and others as innocents in search of the good. We stumble; we falter; we are sometimes mischievous. We are often cantankerous, headstrong, and paradoxical. However, every one of us is a sturdy arrow, born aimed at the proper target. Sometimes we fly true. Sometimes we do not. Compassion makes us, at the very least, bearable to one another while we are learning the mastery of the bow.

Compassion sometimes feels like a good mother's embrace. It scoops up all the wretched stuff and makes everything alright with it, not against it. *Yes, honey, isn't it awful? Let's just sit with that for a moment.*

Compassion has a lot of space in it for things to be as they are. When you have compassion for yourself, you do not feel as much need to be right or wrong. You can just be who you are, learning what you came to learn. And humanity, as it is, cannot rain down a storm of malfeasance upon you. It can only mist you with its is-ness.

Compassion is the understanding that in this life there are no universal answers to the universal questions. When you meet the questions, you peer inside your own experience for the answers that feel meaningful or palliative to you. Compassion allows you to see perspectives where you might have seen only differences.

Compassion is the willingness to leave the judgment or the nonjudgment to others or some higher power and, instead, to hold the struggle itself in the palm and to touch it to the heart.

The dictionary defines the word *strength* using such terms as fortitude, backbone, and durability. But the holy spirit behind the word is vulnerability.

Most of us, maybe all of us, grew up in an environment where we had to be tough to survive. There was a point fairly early in my childhood when I realized, *Oh, okay, nobody's in charge here.* My home was not a place of refuge or fairness. Out of necessity, I put on a two-tone cloak of invisibility and invincibility, and I did not take it off for a very long time.

The problem is that most of us wear our cloaks long past the time when they are needed. We do not understand the damage they cause, and we don't know how to take them off. As children, we have no resources other than the personas we adopt to protect us from the inhospitable world. As we become them and they become us, we lose sight of who we really are. When we are detached from our own authenticity, without a strong sense of self, we readily take on guises that others expect of us.

Now vulnerability is chasing us down like a fast-moving train. This world is not going to let us hide forever. All things must be known and that includes us. At this moment in human history we are all realizing that anything protective, false, or illusory including the masks, roles, and identities has to go. We are in a collective state of disrobing and dismantling.

Obstructing this operation is all the stuff that makes feeling vulnerable so hard. Shame, guilt, trauma, betrayal, fear, abandonment, worthiness. Some of that may be yours from this lifetime, but it also can be assumed from the collective and inherited from ancestors. Regardless of how they became ours, becoming vulnerable allows all these deep wounds to surface. The authentic you is what emerges once they are healed. In this healed state, vulnerability is supplanted with openness and ease, confidence and resiliency.

Vulnerability is the act and state of willingness to be seen as your true self. It is an internal reckoning of your inherent goodness, rightness, and enoughness that radiates outward as an unassailable validity. But at first, it can feel like annihilation.

When you trust enough to walk through the initiatory flames, vulnerability becomes your freedom. When you have nothing to hide, there is nothing to hide from. When who you are needs no justification, and how you choose to live requires no explanation, you are free. No one can make you believe anything you know is not true. No one can force you to act in ways that are inconsistent with how you desire to act. You need no defense, and you need no attack. And though your outer world does not need to reflect your realized sense of self, inevitably it will.

Vulnerability is a decision you make—to show up naked and willing no matter how difficult. And in the exchange, you become the sovereign being you have always been beneath the cloak.

The flocked wallpaper

You've pasted to your being

Is wearing a little thin

It wasn't that thick to begin with

Layers peel

Seams bust

Colors fade

Patterns to dust

No longer fine

Or hiding flaws

Distracting the eye

With its deceptive design

All that is false

Must fall to the ground

For the state of things

To be revealed

Dear Human,
You were born to remember.

To be born human is to be suddenly stripped of our sense of belonging to everything. Our knowing of who we are gets pulled from beneath us like a flashy magician's trick. There we are on day one with all our plates and cups and cutlery appearing orderly with no table in sight.

This inherited forgetting sometimes generates an unwieldy, otherworldly sadness that may not be tied to personal events or circumstances. We may feel misunderstood, overlooked, disappointed, or simply that we do not belong. We might feel lost, alone, or unworthy of something we cannot quite grasp.

Forgetting is such a vague devastation. I was no good at hiding or disguising its unnameable heartbreak. I wore my yearning on the surface like a too-small jacket. From childhood through adulthood, I was plagued by comments like, *cheer up, it's not that bad*; *you look so much prettier when you smile*; and *can't you just be happy?* I knew people thought there was something wrong with me. Sometimes I believed this too, and no strength of will or depth of desire made much of a difference.

But somewhere on the road out of forgetting, I began to sense that there was an assignment buried within my ancient, timeless heart. An itch grew to understand where I was, who I was, and why I was here. Though it often felt like confusion, I came to see it as a fundamental state of curiosity—the most natural of all human conditions. In other words, there was something very right with me.

We were each born with a persistent ambition to unfold the tattered treasure map that is shoved into the pockets of our lives. As we embark on the quest we cannot ignore, we shed layers of illusion and draw ever closer to the ultimate truth—that we are the energy of heaven materialized in matter. No one alike; everyone significant.

Feeling overwhelmed, hopeless, or sad is often just the starter's gun that sets us onto the path of deep self-discovery. The good news is that we are loved so much that in our longing to experience the fullness of being human, we have been granted VIP access to everything that entails. The fine print is that we will experience the fullness of being human. On planet Earth, that means full-body participation in polarity—good/bad, dark/light, right/wrong, rich/poor, life/death.

With the gift of free will, there is much you have to say about your path here, but a lot has been predetermined. What is established is that you are here with special gifts, conditions and lineages. It is as if your soul sat around a conference table with God and made a wish list of what it wanted to explore—the family into which you were born, the abilities that lie in wait, the challenges you would face, and the love you would gain and lose. What has not been decided is the manner in which you will learn from these things.

Accepting that, on a higher level, you chose to be in your life exactly as you are is one of the most difficult things you may ever do, especially if your life has been extra challenging. Every life is challenging, but clearly, some are more so. Although it is never okay for you to be mistreated in any way, it is one of life's great paradoxes that you have the capacity to accept what is and also know it is not acceptable.

When we have difficulty with acceptance, it is not about denial. We have been subjected to loss, injustice, and cruelty. There is no denying that. The difficulty arises when we spend our precious energy trying to wrestle our reality into something it is not rather than owning *how* we choose to experience what life grants us, personal preferences aside.

Taking responsibility means you agree to sit with your life experiences and let them pick you apart a bit, squeeze you, and toss you around until you can see what they have come to teach you. This process is not comfortable or easy, but it will set you on the path of discerning where you need to surrender and where you need to step up.

I once had a difficult encounter with a friend who accused me of many things. It was so tempting to pick up my sword of self-righteousness and start slashing. It would have provided some much-desired, short-term relief, but it would have caused a lot of harm too. It also would have been easier to fall on that sword, smoothing things over by accepting responsibility for things that were not mine to accept. Fortunately, by this time, I already had ruled out the complete avoidance strategy because, well, that never worked.

Instead, I chose to commune with all the feelings that arose—shock, anger, shame, grief. There was a lot. The process took much longer than I wanted it to. But in the end, everything in that conflict taught me something about myself that I really needed to learn. Even though the situation did not turn out as I had hoped, it was a gift I hated and then appreciated.

While you are fully responsible for yourself, you are not responsible for how others react or feel about you and the choices you make. That is their business. Your business is to know what you are responsible for and what you are not. Then you will know how to surrender, how to step up, and that your world has not betrayed you.

Being Human Prayer

Thank you for the full-body experience of being human that I asked for.

Help me to discern between what I am responsible for and what I am not.

Guide me in right action and right inaction.

Let compassion infuse all interactions, with myself and with others.

Lead me through acceptance of what is to the freedom of what can be.

We are not apprentice bricklayers; our walls of self-protection are masterfully built. Our fortresses are old and sturdy enough to keep everything in. And out.

Unfortunately, this means that the walls we think are keeping painful emotions hidden and hurtful weaponry at bay also are preventing us from receiving and expressing a greater depth of love and belonging.

In the homes I have known over the decades, I have always found a place for an enormous corkboard. On it, I pin a hundred or so photos of family and friends. The people pictured are usually smiling or making funny faces for the camera, but of course, much is not revealed. I know for certain their lives have been filled not just with joy but also with sorrow, disappointment, and fear.

We humans are battered by the invisible force of life on Earth. We suffer emotional wounds both subtle and silent in addition to the more blatant ones. As adults, we face a sliding scale of unavoidable affronts from the mildly annoying to the breathtakingly awful.

We do not get through these moments unscathed; we are seriously scathed. You can almost feel your DNA shift as you encounter them. In response, we lay another brick on the wall.

Our defenses have an impressive array of expression including perfectionism, intellectualism, fundamentalism, egoism, sarcasm, humor, disordered eating, self-medication, timidity, defeat, recklessness, aggressiveness, withdrawal, extreme competence—pretty much everything that is not being at ease.

Our everyday state is a combination of woundedness, vigilance, camouflage, and protectionism.

As a society, we have been encamped behind these walls for a good long while. A weary wave of disconnection and numbness has washed over an entire species, and this contributes to actions that are neither loving nor kind.

But hold onto your hats—the crumbling already has begun.

Humanity's destination is unconditional love. There is no stopping us on this journey, and we are well on our way. Being human requires each of us in our own time to remove our walls, brick by brick, and to feel all of our emotions. The breach may bring an overwhelming rush of pain, rage, hopelessness, and betrayal. It may feel like an endless trickle of fear, anxiety, and sadness. Or something in between. The process, as difficult as it may be to experience, is the same for all:

Feel what you feel, no holding back.

Observe and acknowledge what you are feeling.

Express what you are feeling in a way that does no harm.

Love yourself through the experience of each stage, especially when you think you are doing it badly.

Sadly, loving ourselves through our emotional expression does not come naturally. We may hate feeling weak and vulnerable, being such a mess. But ignoring, suppressing, or rejecting our emotions is a refusal not just of our human-ness but of our essential power.

There is a regenerative dynamism in the release of emotional energy that serves our healing. As we heal, we then can witness the emotions of others without becoming triggered into defending ourselves, making it about us, shutting down, or shutting them down.

I am learning this mostly from my grown daughter who does not let me get away with any form of disallowing her feelings. If I am too quick to offer her some alternative way of approaching a situation that might diffuse her feelings, she will stop me midsentence and ask that she be allowed to feel what she feels. I admire this so much and, frankly, cannot fathom where she learned to do it since, clearly, I am still in school.

Despite our good intentions, there is actually no way to help people feel their feelings, and what we might consider to be of help often is a hindrance. The primeval makeup of our emotions is tremendously complex particularly when they seem out of proportion or out of place.

Allowing people to have their feelings gives them the opportunity to permanently clear them from their physical, emotional, mental, and spiritual bodies. This is an incredible gift. You also can learn to respectfully instruct others on how to allow your feelings and to realize that if they cannot do so, the relationship may not be a healthy one. This is a gift to yourself.

Learning to navigate the emotional landscape can be a messy process. We will make mistakes and say the wrong things. The wrong things will be said to us. Emotional intelligence guides us to lovingly recognize the ways in which our defenses are built. Spiritual maturity calls us to recognize the defense mechanisms of others and to be softened by compassion until we all arrive at the unconditional love that is our birthright.

Feelings Formula

$$\frac{\text{Feel} + \text{Observe} + \text{Express} + \text{Love} = \text{Healing}}{\text{Mess up} \times \text{Repeat}}$$

Dear Human,
Trouble is plentiful but purposeful.

In a place where uncertainty is a sure thing, your birth was a risky *Yes* to being human without knowing what that really meant or would bring.

In life, we are continually asked to make decisions without knowing how those decisions will impact us and the people we care about. Most of us want desperately to do the right thing, but we are not allowed to know if things will turn out that way. It seems almost cruel that we cannot guarantee that our good intentions will lead to the good outcomes we desire.

Doubt may seem like a reasonable response to uncertainty, but it is also completely optional. It is nothing more than an energy you can choose to pick up off the banquet table or pass by.

Choosing doubt has a way of stealing the contentment you might feel about a decision you've made and turning it into worry and regret. It can take the resolution you might experience from taking action and turn it into anxiety. And choosing doubt over and over so that it becomes a modus operandi eventually will undermine your confidence. Then, even minor decisions will create unease, and relatively simple situations will exhaust you with their fearful list of unintended consequences.

Or you can choose to trust.

Trust means accepting that life will nudge you toward the things you might not want to experience so you can grow bolder, become softer, gain wisdom, and love better. Trusting yourself is to defer to your intuition, the unfailing inner compass that always points to the right decision. Not necessarily the one that brings roses and candy canes, but the one that will usher in the exact right scenario to serve you and your growth best.

Inevitably, you will face obstacles. You sometimes may need to make amends or double back and choose differently. What you will not have to do is waste your precious energy engaging with the vacuum of doubt that sucks the joy out of living life to the fullest.

Ironically, embracing the unknown washes

you free and clear of fear about the future. It releases you from the small and sometimes faulty ideas you may have about what is possible. When you limit yourself only to what you have known or what you have been told, you disconnect yourself from the magic of composing something completely new and as yet unknowable.

In the present moment, you are both the creator of your reality and are living in the flow of the divine plan for all that is. It is only here that you can fold into the unfolding mystery of life. It is here you will know that all roads lead to your rise.

When I first started learning about codependency, I thought it was a term used to describe toxic relationships where boundaries are often breached and enabling is the prevailing behavior. I did not think it applied to me. Even as my understanding of it grew, I continued to assume it was either not that common or not that serious. But now I believe otherwise.

Codependency is really about the conditions we place around love. It is present when our ability to love people depends on who they are, how they behave, or what they believe. It is present when we feel we must change who we are, how we behave, or what we believe to be loved.

In the extreme, codependency can be almost pathological. But far more subtle expressions of it can be just as damaging, perhaps even more so since they often fly under the radar.

Codependency is passed down to us along ancestral lines as a survival instinct. Our primary relationships are so fundamental to our basic needs that we must take the love that is offered regardless of whether it is conditional or not. We become so programmed to love and be loved conditionally that we come to believe that conditions are necessary and perfectly appropriate.

The problem is that being loved conditionally deteriorates our sense of self-worth. Deep within, perhaps even unconsciously, we may begin to feel that we are not good enough to be loved as we are. We start to believe that we have to be somebody we are not in order to be loved at all. By loving others with conditions, we inadvertently damage the self-worth of the ones we love, even if it is not our intent.

My imperfect parents loved me conditionally. I am learning to love unconditionally, but I am not perfect either. Now that I am more aware, it is almost comical how often I get caught in codependent quagmires like this one:

Son: I might not be able to come home for Christmas.

Me: That's going to break my heart.

Son: Mom, you can't say that!

Me: Damn, you're right; that's so codependent.

Son: (Smiles victoriously.)

I also have noticed, with pained embarrassment, the slight adjustments I might make to my style, speech, or gestures depending on who I am interacting with and whether or not I am hoping they will like me.

If I am being honest, I have to admit that loving conditionally is at the root of all my relationship problems with the people I love most and is the source of every resentment they might have toward me. And if they have not been loved for who they are, completely free of conditions, they are justified in feeling that way.

This does not make me a terrible person. It just means that I have thoroughly investigated these relationships and taken responsibility for my part in what they are and are not. This has been both hard and heartbreaking. By comparison, it was much easier for me to acknowledge and forgive others, especially my parents, for loving me conditionally. So perhaps, one day, I will be granted clemency. Perhaps I already have been.

Breaking the cycle of codependency and moving toward unconditional love is to become the observer of yourself in your relationships. Notice the ways you try to control people's behavior or get them to be other than who they are. Recognize the ways you might have changed yourself for others, and consider if this has made you feel unworthy of the love you deserve. Can you acknowledge that you deserve unconditional love even if you did not get it or are not getting it now?

Unlearning codependency is a boots-on-the-ground operation that plays itself out in daily life, so there are plenty of opportunities to practice. As you recalibrate, remember to be kind to yourself and others. Know that even your steps backward are taking you one step closer to unconditional love.

As a Catholic schoolgirl, I had lots of ideas about good and bad, guilt and innocence, heaven and hell.

At the root of it all was the teaching that I was born bad and had to earn back God's favor by my expiration date *or else*. And that everything I did between birth and death would get logged into two columns labeled Good or Evil, tallied on the last day to land me in heaven or hell.

Guilt was almost always top-of-mind. If I did anything wrong, I felt I was aggrieving God. And every time I did something good, I hoped it was enough to make up for the bad. To help my case, I would only say prayers of gratitude and devotion, never of wishes and pleas. The pressure of this construct was way too much for me to bear. Eventually, I felt I had just two options: 1) Suffer under this torturous system or 2) Toss out the whole system—no God, no pressure.

I tried to rid myself of the guilt the only way I knew how—by turning away from the sacred nature of my life. Unfortunately, that did not banish the guilt. It only fractured me from the truth of my being, leaving the underlying longing for spiritual connection intact. In other words, I now felt guilty *and* lost. What a party-pooping, mojo-crushing joy-killer.

I now think of guilt as a false program installed in our software that keeps us from experiencing the full grandeur of our being. Primarily, it keeps us from knowing ourselves as aspects of God that cannot, by design, be faulty. Guilt cuts us off from our inner guidance, which fosters tentativeness in fear of judgment. It keeps us from learning from our mistakes because disappointing God is too painful a prospect.

When guilt is used by others as a tool to assess our goodness, it keeps us from knowing we are inherently good. When it is used to keep us in line, it disguises our alignment to our rightness.

You are divinity itself, exploring itself as you. Because you have been cast from unconditional love, you are loved unconditionally. Everything you do, think, say, believe, and experience is seen through the eyes of unconditional love.

When you understand yourself to be unconditional love, you begin to act in ways that are loving. When you act in loving ways, you are able to apologize if needed, correct yourself when necessary, and forgive all parties. When you know yourself to be loved unconditionally, you are unable to judge others because you know they are loved like that too.

Guilt is fake, and you are real.

Guilt Manifesto

I'm done with you.

Fear has been part of the human experience for a very long, horrible time. Its creepy, crooked fingers reach far into our perspectives and decisions with persistent and persuasive lies. But truth be told, fear is nothing more than a shadow puppet climbing up the bedroom wall of life—an illusory pretender.

Nothing feels more real than fear, especially the deep fears that plunge us into survival mode:

sudden oncoming traffic

grave diagnoses

encounters with grizzlies

The "lesser" but no-less influential fears are the everyday anxieties we face:

falling ill

losing a relationship

raising children

making ends meet

facing uncomfortable stuff

meeting new people

growing old

managing life

Even if you know it is irrational, fear can keep you frozen in situations that are not good for you or trapped in thinking patterns that are not healthy. Or nice. Or fun.

It is important to recognize that a lot of the fear you may experience is not a direct result of the life you are leading, nor is it coming from a failure of character or flaw in your makeup. There are forces at play here on Earth that have sought to keep humans in the powerlessness of fear. When we are exhausted mentally, physically, and spiritually by living in and running from fear, we tend to seek fixes, comfort, and protection outside of ourselves. This outward-faced seeking weakens our ability to tap inner resources and opens us up to external influence.

But regardless of the origins, fear is something everyone will experience and eventually must face.

The human collective is moving into a higher-vibrational reality. This is the process of both individual and collective ascension. Because fear is a low vibrational energy, it cannot exist at the higher frequencies. As a result, the fear that is being held in your physical body and your energy body must be released as you ascend. Same goes with the fear held in the collective consciousness. It must come up and out as we ascend. What I have learned, however, is that fear cannot stand up to the scrutiny of our loving attention.

I have been controlled by my fears. Layers of fear. Rooms of fear. Worlds of fear. I went through a period of 24/7 panic attacks that were so severe I barely slept for months. I was on the verge of a breakdown when I finally went to see my doctor. Without much discussion, he gave me one prescription for depression and one for anxiety, and I headed straight for the drugstore. But despite my desperate desire for relief, I just did not see how that was going to solve anything. I stepped out of line and headed home. Over the next several months, I changed everything about how I was living my life. I removed caffeine and alcohol from my routine, committed to yoga and meditation practices, turned off the TV, and turned away from obligations and people who filled me with dread. I spent more time on things that brought me peace and joy, and as a result, I found reprieve from the heart-pounding, palm-sweating existence I had been living. But the underlying fears lingered.

One day, as I sat in meditation, I began to feel the panic rising again. I was so depleted by my inability to stem the tide of fear, I could see nothing left to do but surrender. There was nothing more to say but, *Just kill me already. I have no fight left.* I waved the white flag and let the fear wash over and through me, expecting to be overcome. Instead, the fear that had felt so debilitating simply evaporated.

This was not a one and done event. But the more fear I faced, the less power it had over me. Much of it was merely illusion. It did not make sense that while I was safe, healthy, and loved, my vital signs were stuck in fight or flight mode. Facing my fears, at a pace I could handle, eventually led me to the deepest questions—who am I, where am I, and why am I?

These questions are intimately coupled to our most acute fears. And answering them for ourselves is the ultimate antidote. Everyone is different. Some people are processing our collective fear as part of their soul mission. Others are dealing with the terror of long-buried trauma. And sometimes this is far more than anyone should be asked to handle. So each person's path with fear should be honored and respected including the decision to seek whatever kind of support is needed from traditional to nontraditional therapy, plant medicine to medication. Although there is no one correct way to process fear, all fear is neutralized by feeling it.

Because our collective ascension has reached a powerful and unstoppable momentum, our fears are being presented for clearing like a drenching, equatorial rain. Still, the resolution remains the same. Let yourself feel the fear in the way that best honors your beautiful worthiness.

Without a doubt, this is a heroic path. Eventually you will know that while walking through fear is a very difficult experience, you are a boundless being, of infinite power, being supported by the never-ending field of loving light. More than anything, remember that the destination now in our sights is a reality free from fear.

I still experience fear at times, but it is no longer terrifying. And it is definitely not paralyzing. For years now, my mantra has been: *I'm afraid, and I'm going anyway.* This allows me to feel the way I feel and not let it beat me into stagnation. I want to live the biggest, boldest, most alive life I can live, and retreating in fear does not allow for that. As I have become more accustomed to walking through my fears or sometimes just ignoring them, like you do when ziplining or bungee jumping, I have found a way to get cozy with the discomfort of fear. And I cannot deny that being in that place also feels very alive. Like, *whoa—I'm alive—and I hate it! But also, look at me doing this thing I never thought I would do.*

Support for Fear

To get to the peace and joy that is your birthright, you will have to walk through the experience of facing and feeling your fears. No one can do that for you. But you do not have to do it without help. My methods were right for me. Your methods should be right for you. Please seek whatever creative approach or professional help you require and do not stop until you find the support you deserve.

You are loved.

Our lives are built on myths and wounds
But we are not our lives
We are made of sun and moon
Wave and particle and desire.
Bound up in silver thread
Each disabled heart
Winds back to its original spool
Where love becomes unfurled.

Dear Human,
Be the target of your love bomb.

Self-love is the miracle cure that heals wounds, rights wrongs, and brings disequilibrium into alignment. This powerful antidote is free, abundant, and easily accessible. So why does this medicine, at times, feel beyond our reach and impossible to take?

Throughout the ages, we have experienced many shades of darkness. We have suffered a multitude of traumas. The resulting feelings of shame, blame, and pain can complicate our relationship with ourselves.

Long after the damage has been done either to us or by us, our internal dialogue continues to be the driver of the feelings that block us from receiving our own love. We have to re-learn how to be in a healthy relationship with ourselves, which is begun by connecting with the innocence and purity within. This is the holy part of us that is untouchable, unchanging, and incorruptible but has nonetheless experienced difficult things.

Your life—with its highs and lows—is constantly showing you where your loving attention is required. It is the internal guidance system that helps you determine what loving action is needed now, whether it be compassion, tears, rage, rest, truth, humility, courage, support, prayer, forgiveness, or responsibility. It will whisper:

> *Please place your spotlight on this.*
>
> *Your tears are needed there.*
>
> *What can you own rather than blame?*
>
> *Witness rather than ignore?*
>
> *Can you apply a little forgiveness to this?*
>
> *Would you spread a little joy on that?*

If you aren't listening, your life will begin to raise a ruckus you can't ignore. It will shout:

> *How does losing your job really make you feel?*
>
> *What does this betrayal help you understand about yourself?*

Maybe this injury will help you slow down.

Perhaps this breakdown will encourage your reflection.

I have learned to make my way into healing through self-love by treating myself as I would an innocent child. I remind myself that no matter what I encounter, my feelings are valid, it is okay to feel and express them, and I am worthy of my own love even if I don't believe I deserve it. I have not found a single wound too stubborn or severe for this treatment, though sometimes the protocol goes on for years.

When I have been wronged, I focus not on the perpetrator but on my innocent self and the hurt or shame I am touching into. When I have done wrong, I focus my love first on the innocent self who must have had a reason for acting this way and the resulting feelings of regret or righteousness. If action is called for later, it can then come from a more healed place. This is how we parent our inner child through the most difficult ordeals.

One common pitfall is thinking that because you are experiencing so much pain, you must not know how to heal or have not done it correctly. Why don't you feel better, happier? The truth is that you are healing, but there is a lot to heal.

I was sitting on a sand dune overlooking Lake Michigan when I suddenly understood how nature was holding me like a mother through my most willful periods of victimhood, self-sabotage, and inner loathing. Since then, I have let many things parent me. Music, sun, quiet, birdsong, friends, clean sheets, a familiar chair, my skin, a hot soup.

One of the loveliest side effects of self-love is that it compels in us a greater compassion for others. Loving ourselves creates a ripple effect that makes the world a better, more healed place. If the world's dissonance causes suffering for you, remember it does so because you are viewing it from a more healed place where the dissonance is no longer tolerable. There was a time when humanity could not see its own anguish. It was just suffering and causing more misery as a result.

There may be no more arduous course of treatment in life than to love oneself. It often feels more like a battle than a cure. It might be the final skirmish before we reach the foreign shore of unconditional love. Nonetheless, no matter what you face on your life path, self-love can be your compass, your flashlight, your trail map, your walking stick, your sturdy shoes, your backpack, and your sunblock.

If there were only one way to be winning as a human, it would be through the love you lavish upon yourself. The difficulty of that task will teach you everything you came to learn. Mastering it will take you everywhere you want to go.

Prior to the spring of 2020, when the global population retreated to their homes, I didn't think it was possible for people to slow down. Until we were forced off the collective treadmill, our history had been heading into hyperdrive. Life was becoming a tightening coil of stress, fatigue, and forward momentum so that by the time we reach middle age—or maybe even middle school—we are a hot mess of unresolved tension.

Like it or not, we've been unplugged from the external world of tasks and social obligations. From here, we can better see that living outside of nature, in opposition to intrinsic cycles of growth and rest, has been creating a phenomenon of mass exhaustion, lifelessness, and despondency. Detachment from stimuli has become so foreign that for some it is seriously unsettling.

In addition to all the peripheral noise, human consciousness is expanding at an unprecedented rate. The energy field within and around us is speeding up, vibrating at higher and higher frequencies. Our bodies, down to the subcellular level, are constantly working to adapt to these upgrades even as they are pressed to mitigate increasing environmental toxicity.

It's no wonder that our weariness feels next-level or seems to come out of nowhere at times.

From within the collateral damage of mass quarantine, we have been gifted a moment to become reacquainted with the long-forgotten fertile dormancy. The sacred pause, if we care to see it that way.

Our ascension path into higher vibrations will not abate. It will become increasingly important to give ourselves permission to rest and to learn to rest deeply *while* the world spins around us. Cultivating a state of calm awareness as our default setting creates the neutrality that has been described in the Bible as *the peace that passeth all understanding.*

This peace has a pace all its own—that of harmony and heaven. It is accessible to all through the in-between spaces such as the ones that bridge the inhale and exhale and lead us from doing into being. Just these two deceptively simple things, breathing and being, are acts of rebellion against the force of progress, the constant onward march. Our gentle insurgency would mean saying *no, thank you* to everything that wants to press into the next thing and *yes, please* to everything that allows us to disintegrate into the right now. To pause here is to drop all agendas and ride the current of enchantment that threads its way through every present moment.

There will be seconds, maybe even longer, when everything softens. To linger there is to let the moment teach you how to love your life.

Rest Meditation

Sit or lie so you will be comfortable for a little while. Set a timer for no longer than five minutes.

Let gravity pull you toward the Earth's core.

Let go of all resistance.

Bring your attention to the rim of your nostrils and feel the breath moving in and out. With each inhale, feel the coolness of the breath. With each exhale, release tension from your entire body.

When your breathing grows comfortable, draw your focus to the empty space of nothingness between each inhale and exhale. It may be just a split second. Linger lightly in those spaces without creating strain in the breath.

Repeat daily if possible, increasing the time if your body, mind and spirit call for more.

Landscapes of white fabric
Door ajar to the misty morning,
Is there a prayer more sacred
Than staying in bed?
Hammers double-tick in the distance
Birds and buses about their business
Plans happening
People intent on living, despite.
I am not needed
Not necessary except to myself
Life occurs eventually
In my ears and for my eyes.
I don't take the moment lightly
Or squander the sweetness
I call in a world of Heaven
Only for all, and forever.

It does not take long for isolated people to miss the touch of other humans. We are bees in a hive, trees in a stand. Like them, we are beings of energy, meant to be lifted, balanced, and swayed by the energy of others. Through our proximity and touch, we exchange unseen things. We do not learn this, but we feel it.

I would marvel when my former husband, who would never admit to an awareness of energy, would occasionally say when I walked in the door, *What's wrong?*, when I had not even taken off my coat.

After my children were grown and out in the world, I spent a lot of time alone. This was necessary for me to regain the familiarity of my energy and essence, but I sometimes missed the touch of other humans. I was in a stage of deep self-healing, so my own touch became critical for my well-being. Rituals I developed during that time still serve me today. They link my spirit to my body and my body to the Earth, creating a toroidal loop of connectedness that allows me to be at home no matter where I am or with whom.

Ritual is the honor we bestow on the extraordinary gifts of ordinary life. These moments, made reverent by persistent attention, are the temple gates through which we enter the sacred nature of all things. Ritual allows us to feel a sense of belonging in the shapeless space of our lives and to create a sanctuary outside of time and chaos.

My favorite rituals are simple, fleeting, and make sense only to me. Before my feet hit the floor each morning I fill my lungs with conscious breath to inflate my day with courage and strength. I light a candle at breakfast to represent the sacred fire that endures within me. I pause as the sun casts shadows across the snow to appreciate the miracle of warm against cold. I listen for the lake's roar. Turn my face to the wind. I touch my food and tell it I am grateful.

As soothing as these rituals are, they cannot take the place of physical connection with friends and family. Touch takes our energetic alliance with all of life and magnifies it. You know this if you have ever offered a compassionate touch to a stranger's elbow in a moment of sorrow, cupped the corner of your lover's jaw in a gesture of acceptance, or placed the back of your hand against a hot forehead. You know this if you have felt the absurd hopefulness of a child's sticky, sweaty palm in yours.

This sensory interaction with life itself distinguishes our human experience in form in an existence that is primarily not of form. To feel life through the senses is a precious gift of inestimable value.

Sometimes I wonder, what if this were my only human lifetime, or my last? What would I want to experience? I think I would want to touch someone with great care and presence and to experience that sacred collaboration as it ripples into infinity.

Chapel chime, call to prayer

Cats purring at closed doors

Coffee mugs clinking teeth

Commuter trains with worker bees

Hey neighbor behind windows across the
courtyard—

Do you hear what I hear,

Some consecrated sound breaking into
presence?

What if our arms were like rubber

Stretching across that brick expanse.

Could we link up, sync up,

Toast and tell stories of our broken hopes?

Dear Human,
The road to freedom is paved with
broken rules.

If your life could give you one gift, it would be to help you understand that no one has authority over you and that you are the only authority you will ever need.

We live in a society in which we have almost no authority in our own lives. We were born to parents who likely went well beyond the minimal requirements for keeping us safe, healthy, and loved. We learned early to acquiesce to their desires for us, which created thought patterns and behaviors that adhered to their parameters of acceptability. We go on to be influenced by teachers, coaches, physicians, religious figures, bosses, marketers, and government leaders with a vested interest in controlling how we think and behave. Along the way, we have been convinced that this is for our own good. Out of concern, and fear, we pass this conditioning on to our children, which, unfortunately, has made them easier to control. This highly efficient trickle-down dynamic creates systems of control that are virtually invisible to the people in their grip.

We may have given away our authority to such a degree that we no longer know who we truly are, what we want for ourselves, and what we are entitled to. Further, we have been led to believe that we do not have the expertise to know what is right and good for us. But we do.

You are the only one who knows what is right and good for you. Cultivating your intuition, you can tap into universal wisdom to get the information you need to make the best decisions. Your body, with its constant and certain feedback, is your greatest ally. Its divinely inspired operating instructions are simple: What feels right and good *is* right and good. What makes you feel uneasy, unsure, afraid, sick, and disconnected is not.

It naturally follows that once you accept that you are your only authority, you must then own how you are living your life. You cannot live differently or better if you do not take responsibility for your role in what currently exists. And, you cannot heal what you haven't yet acknowledged. Authority is best friends with ownership.

While I was going through the process of uncoupling, I often was tempted to create a list in my mind of everything my then-husband had done wrong. But this was keeping me from owning what I was responsible for, so instead, I made a list about me. It made me look petty and imperfect, and I absolutely hated looking at it. But this step propelled me into ownership, which then advanced me into authority. I forgave myself for what I was complicit in creating and started to examine the things I found more difficult to forgive.

Accepting ownership was both empowering and terrifying. Empowering because I knew that my life could potentially become what I truly wanted it to be. Terrifying because I had to accept that a lot of the hard things I grappled with throughout the years were of my own making. Everything in me wanted to make someone else responsible for my life, so that was bitter medicine.

Many years ago, I was called into the school principal's office where I was met by my child's teacher and a social worker. They began to discuss my child's behavior and their concern. I sat there stunned and speechless as it dawned on me that this was a third-grade intervention.

My ego flared quick and hot like a struck match. My first instinct was to blame and protect, even as my heart wanted the best outcome for my child. But rather than burn the house down, I let it be a lightbulb moment for me.

I knew I had two choices—to become defensive and maybe even accusatory or to take responsibility for having played a role in creating the situation. I opted for ownership, which meant taking a long, hard look at how I was parenting. This was one of the most difficult things I've ever had to do. I was ashamed and crushed over the damage I had caused. And I had to summon the courage to admit to my mistakes and change course. Today, that child is an exceptional human being who has overcome much of my deficient parenting. We have a relationship I truly treasure. But if I am being honest, forgiving myself is an ongoing project that still challenges me.

Claiming ownership and authority in our own lives is not just about the magnificent march toward sovereignty. It is also about the path of humility, honesty, and forgiveness. It is always surprising to me that the latter requires even more fortitude than the former.

When I first understood that I had been heavily conditioned, a cold chill washed through me at the thought of being manipulated by some invisible enemy. But time helped me see that the alarm was more about freedom than it was about control. In my mind's eye, I saw the cell doors suddenly being flung open, a weary prison guard chucking the keys at my chest mumbling *good luck, sucker* under his breath. I was really on my own, responsible for aspects of myself that I did not know I was not in control of.

My love affair with freedom did not begin with some splashy, sexy desire to become someone wild and limitless or to do something audacious and daring. Uh, no. It began timidly with a modest little prayer: *Please, freedom, help me know who the hell I am and what it is I even want because right now, I do not.*

This seemed like a tragedy to me—that I was not even free enough to imagine a dream to dream. I had the sensation that there was a tarp over my life that looked like the sky but did not allow me to see the true potential of my own humanity, just like *The Truman Show*. I felt as if I had been slotted into the confines of a certain life that came with invisible parameters established by others of how to think, act, and be. From the beginning, my orientation to life, which I knew should face inward, was constantly drawn outward into a tangled mess of too much everything and not enough something.

My route to freedom seems to be walking me through all the ways in which I am not yet free so that I can see what needs to be undone, cast off, broken through.

These are necessary steps to the threshold of true freedom, which, like grace or joy is not a destination. It is a state of everlasting expansion into greater levels of freedom. And while it is tempting to view this as an outward-reaching experience in which freedom is racked up like tokens in a video game, the exquisite endowment of life on Earth is that it is actually a return, amid all the nonsense of existence, to the truth of you.

The truth is that the heart of God is beating in your chest, and the breath of sacred life is filling your lungs. Once you know that, nothing can keep you from your birthright—the freedom that resides within. It is untouchable by outside influence and carries your power to create the life you want.

My budding independence became a process of discovering what and who was influencing my thoughts and beliefs about things on a very deep level.

What does it mean to be me outside of what society has programmed?

What do I believe my purpose is beyond what has been prescribed by others?

What does it mean to be authentic in a world where facades and personas are the norm?

Who am I responsible to and for, and what are my responsibilities exactly?

What is true here, and what is veiled or distorted?

What happens when my beliefs come crashing down around me—how do I rebuild?

Even now, after years of unearthing layer upon layer of conditioning, the questions keep coming because in truth, there will always be more that is unknown than known. Self-scrutiny has become a way of life. The question I ask most often now is, *What is the wisdom of my inner knowing telling me?*

Independence is the acceptance of our value and power. It is a continual turning away from the throbbing mass of constant input into who we are and remembering to turn inward for the understanding, guidance, and endurance to act according to our own code of honor in the face of everyone else's desires and demands.

Once the snowball effect kicks in, you will be astonished at how quickly the layers of conditioning slough off revealing a clarity and peace the old way of life never offered. Fair warning—there will be no turning back. You cannot unknow what you know once you know it. For better or worse, the Independence Equation is:

Truth + Responsibility = Change.

You will be changed fundamentally by the process and that inevitably means some things—beliefs, situations, relationships, ways of being—no longer will fit.

Independence is the freedom you unlock for yourself. No one has the keys but you. When there is no one and nothing standing between your mind, your heart, and your choices, you are omnipotent in your life. What an audacious and daring thing.

Dear Human,
Let life change you.

Assumptions are like your kitchen junk drawer—filled with unnecessary and unhelpful items that persist in hanging around despite their uselessness. I have never been pleasantly surprised by assumptions I have made, but I am increasingly, acutely aware of their hidden agendas.

Assumptions often conceal our unwillingness to show up to situations naked, disarmed, and open. And this is what happens when we let go of assumptions. We arrive at each encounter like a blank slate, ready and willing to accept what is now, not what we believe is or what was. I think this might be the best possible way to honor the one in front of you—by starting with the knowing that they are completely new to you in every moment, to show up with an innocent curiosity instead of preconceived notions. With questions instead of answers. Who are you right now? What are you thinking? How are you feeling? What shall we be to each other in this instant?

Even the person you were brushing your teeth with twenty minutes ago is no longer that person. And neither are you. Not assuming you know who they are, what they are thinking, and how they will behave is a big and boundless gift that allows them to be completely themselves, without expectations, free from the burden of former selves and past actions.

And what if you were able to let go of assumptions you have of yourself? What possibilities would unfurl if there were no grooved road predetermining your destination? What sweet lightness and greater freedom could you experience?

Inevitably, this beautiful practice of being a blank slate compels us to let go of our stringent ideas about the nature of truth and to accept the freewheeling fun of knowing something anew.

Thinking of right as the opposite of wrong has gotten me into a world of trouble. The kind of trouble that splits friends and lovers and families and nations and peoples. My ideas about right and wrong were placing conflict and judgment at the center of my experience, and I no longer desired to live that way. I had to come to a new and more nuanced understanding about rightness, and I gradually began to comprehend it as the observance and acceptance, maybe even love, of all that is—even the things I would rather not observe or accept, and definitely not love.

Life on Earth is an experiential laboratory that creates endless learning opportunities. We have been given free rein to explore everything from dense and dark consciousnesses to high vibrational light frequencies. Our explorations have created injustice and atrocities as well as magic and beauty. We have suffered and enjoyed the consequences of our actions.

But the journey from dark to light is not a

journey from wrong to right. It is the walk from suffering to love.

Polarity is a structure or frame of reference through which we have learned about life. We have learned about peace from war, acceptance from rejection, abundance from poverty. This has been painful but effective. Now humanity is expanding beyond the need to learn through polarity. We are graduating into an awareness of the goodness of everything—even polarity—because of the opportunities it afforded us. Let's just say that we learned about polarity as high school juniors. Just as we don't judge juniors for needing junior year, we don't need to judge ourselves or one another for needing to learn through polarity. Now that we are seniors, there are new classes on the schedule. We finally may be ready to learn about peace from greater peace, love from sweeter love, abundance from abundance flowing.

Rightness Reflection

Have you ever felt so embattled by ideas of right and wrong that you have had to turn away from people you wanted to love or been left feeling angry, disheartened, or lonely? It often is our tight grip on ideas of right and wrong that cuts off circulation to our heart. What if, for a moment, you could release all of that turmoil into the great unknowable mystery of life? To be humble enough to ask that the burden of infallibility be lifted from you. To bless you with the innocence of acceptance of all you cannot know.

How to get to the state of grace—
First, assume you have the heart of God
The child's heart
The rapturous heart
So go there
And never leave
The state of grace will find you
It will pick up its borderless borders
Fold up its old-fashioned road map
Into the shape of an origami rose
Lay it over your heart
And let itself unfold

Honesty is the ever-appearing crossroads that always calls us into greater communion with our true self.

In every moment, you must decide whether you will be who you really are. In this way, honesty is a *Yes* you say to yourself. Honesty is your ability to align with your truth without demanding that others understand or comply with it.

It is a cobbled road, like the ancient Nakasendo Way I trekked in Japan, flanked with sacred shrines and laid with large, uneven boulders. I had to walk slowly and mindfully, considering every step in the split second before it was taken, deciding whether it was steady and true.

Walking the way of honesty is not always easy to do in a fast-paced world that demands constant interaction. If you are disconnected from yourself, you may fall back on automated responses that reflect untruths or half-truths or just not knowing. The price you pay for a misalignment to your truth is high because the harm you can cause to yourself often is greater than the harm you might cause to another.

In my life, I was being unfair and maybe even unloving to another when I stayed in a relationship beyond what I knew was best for me. But I was slowly suffocating myself by dishonoring my worth and nullifying my truth. Concealing my honesty beneath justifications and delaying it with denials was a painful perjury against myself. I had to learn this the hard way.

Life is the force pushing you from below and pulling you from above to flower as you are. Not as a geranium if you are a nasturtium. Not as a blade of grass if you are a tree. You were encoded with your truth long before your birth, as all of nature is, and your commission is to be revealed. Petal by petal, leaf by leaf, moment by moment.

Dear Human,
You must be expressed.

I used to think our stories were not that important. I once believed that the only thing that mattered was the present moment and that in that moment resides the great blissful nothing. But I have come to understand that the present moment also holds every wonderous tale—told and untold. I now know that our stories are the key with which we unlock ourselves and our reasons for being. How we feel about our stories tells us where we are on our journey to experience everything we came to reclaim, resolve, and rectify. So, in a way, our stories are everything.

Our stories—our lives—reveal our still-open wounds, like themes, that need to be told and healed. Each aspect of our story has the potential to lead us deep into the heartbreak that represents the fears, betrayals, and sorrows we have with ourselves and with life. Telling our story is medicine. Listening well to the story of another is a devotional practice as powerful as prayer.

When my daughter was very young, she talked a lot. If she was awake, she was talking. Around that time, I attended a workshop in which the instructor delivered a truth I could not deny. He said that people who talk a lot do not feel heard. On one level, this is obvious, but it struck me deeply. My daughter was born into a very busy household where there already were three young boys. Safe to say, it was fairly difficult for anything or anyone to really be heard. But I did not want to let that reality keep me from addressing her need to be heard, for her story to be told.

Good listening requires presence, which means dropping all your storylines for a minute so you can become absorbed in what the other person is saying. It requires a quiet mind so that you are not distracted by the great chatter of living and your own need to be heard.

I was not especially good at listening until I started wanting to be. Over time, I found that when I really listened, people's tragic, beautiful, grace-filled lives began to unfurl like a big flag on a tall pole. Some people have never told their stories to anyone. Some have talked but never felt heard. Some use surface words to hint at the rooted truths or need big stretches of silence before speaking at all.

The quieter I became, the more clearly I could see how telling the story had the potential to heal the teller. And the more I bore witness to the narratives, the greater my capacity to be the nonjudgmental receptacle for their words of pain, shame, grief, courage, and love.

There are miracles in these stories and sharing them is a sacred exchange. I have a young friend who told me recently that listening to people is his spirituality. This sounded a bell at the core of my being. What more holy observance is there than hearing the story of how God became the one in front of you?

Quiet Mind Meditation

Sit comfortably with a straight spine, on the floor, in a chair, or up against a wall for comfort if needed. Relax your body especially your shoulders, belly, and hips. Observe the rise and fall of your breath for a few minutes, trying not to control it too much. Then, imagine that your brain is a heavy muscle like the quadriceps. Let it soften and relax into the cradle of your skull. With every exhale, let your brain soften more. Watch thoughts float by without letting your focus grab onto them. Keep softening the physical brain and notice how that softens the mind as well. Become aware of the feeling of a soft, quiet mind as if you are fixing the sensation of it into your memory. Stay in this relaxed state for as long as you like. Practice as often as you can. Then, bring your relaxed mind to your next listening experience.

Writing has a way of freeing the mind from the constructs that keep us from expressing our sequestered feelings and darkest thoughts. Somehow, the pen or the keyboard takes the mind offline so that a channel opens between the heart and the surface. The more we write, the more we unearth. When you set down your weighty words, you light a flare that signals you are ready to hear truth and receive healing. It is your acceptance of the divine wisdom that wants to be expressed to and through you. You start the flow of that which you most long to know.

Forget about purpose. Purpose here would be a preposterous trap. When you write, write only for yourself, not for some imagined audience. Write as if those pages will be burned by some kindly ghost at the appropriate moment. Or better yet, as if the words will morph from spits of fury, doubt, and grief into droplets of love, gentleness, and gratitude, which, by grace, they will. Treat your pen as your sword or surgeon's scalpel or the explorer's compass. Let it vanquish fears and foreign lands. Put all of your illness into the writing, like a prescription, and then watch it become the medicine.

Writing has a way of unclogging stuck things—maybe unspeakable things. The words are put into the basket of one of those Chinese lanterns that are lit and launched on warm summer evenings. Though they rise like sacred specters and then vanish into the thin air, somehow, we know our words do not disappear. They are alchemized into ribbons of gold sun and pale moon.

Writing Exercise

Write a letter that will never be sent. Fill it with your rantings, heartbreak, wonder, and joy. Write a poem that will never be published. Let your brilliant nonsense spill onto the page. Write a memoir that will never be read. Know that the writing of you is the work of art no one else could craft.

In 2011 I was hired by a studio to teach yoga before I finished my certification and before I felt ready. By then I had become accustomed to saying yes to things that scared me.

Knowing that what I understood about the ancient art of yoga would always be dwarfed by what there was to know gnawed at my confidence. Almost from day one, I noticed a peculiar phenomenon. Throughout the class, I often would need to clear my throat. I assumed the cause was nerves or that there was something in the environment, maybe a little mold or dust. I was always fine both before and after class.

After nearly a year at that studio, I left to open my own studio where I taught several classes a week. Although I believed passionately in the many gifts of yoga, I continued to grapple with confidence issues. Perhaps more interestingly, I still had the throat condition. After three and a half years of teaching, I decided to step away and just run the studio. I told my staff and students that I did not have sufficient time to both teach and run the studio well. What I did not tell them was that I was not teaching yoga the way I longed to. And I suspected that this was contributing to my throat constriction. I wanted to teach yoga as a spiritual practice, as a way of entering and honoring the sacred temple of the body, connecting to God both within and without, but at the time, I could not even utter the G-word. So I just quit teaching.

Soon after, I started to develop a recurring rash on the front of my neck. Over many months, I made all kinds of adjustments to my diet. Some helped, but none were a cure. I was doing a massive amount of inner work at the time, dealing with a host of challenging stressors. I began to suspect the issue might be energetic, involving the throat chakra, the one related to speaking your truth. But the cliché nature of this had me rolling my own eyes.

In the summer of 2018, I traveled to Peru with a group of friends and yogis. I knew before departing that it would be a transformative experience, and, as if on cue, my body began preparing in undeniable ways. On the flight to Lima, my neck began to redden and itch. Throughout the trip, the rash worsened though I was eating organic, vegan food and drinking purified water. By the final day of the trip, two raw and angry lines spanned the width of my neck. I was supremely uncomfortable. On that last day, I had a session scheduled with a shaman. During the treatment, which included massage, energy work, chanting, dry-brushing, sound vibration, and other techniques, I had a vision. In the vision, I was a 13-year-old girl, a young and rare female initiate into an ancestral shamanic lineage. My father was there with a group of elders, observing as I was being strangled. I would later learn that long ago, shamanic initiates would be brought to the point of crossing over so that they could bear witness to it.

After the treatment, the shaman looked at me rather nonchalantly and said in her patchwork English, *Your heart is not connected to your head.*

I felt a rage rise up from my feet as if the ground around me had been struck by lightning. I do not know if it was the casual way she said it, the bored look on her face like she had seen it all before, or the fact that—hello—I had just been strangled, but I was angry. She knew it and stood firm, refusing to take on whatever was leaching from my system. Clearly, she was not new to this. Beneath the fury, I felt utter defeat and misery that she did not understand how much work I already had done. But she was right. My heart was not connected to my head. My heart was with God. My head and the voice that sprang from it could not admit it.

By the time I landed back home in Chicago, the rash, miraculously, had vanished. I wish I could say it was gone forever, but that was not the case.

Like many people in the spiritual community, I came up through traditional religion. I did not see any way to break away from its oppressive, patriarchal teachings without also walking away from God, so I walked away. Eventually, while my head was preoccupied with other things, my heart meandered its way back. I slowly began to speak and write using veiled terms such as the divine, universe, source. Words my head could tolerate.

As I have continued on my prolonged journey to merge my head with my heart, I am growing more courageous about speaking my truth. My truth is that I believe in God. I believe that everything is God. The rash, not surprisingly, is all but gone.

I first started digging for my truth with a little garden trowel. But to excavate all the layers of familial, religious, and societal conditioning, I had to call in the big guns—first a shovel, then a damn backhoe. It has not been easy or quick, but it has been thorough.

Now, I can speak and write the word *God* and feel only the slightest resistance. I am a work in progress; the voice of God is still learning to speak as me.

No matter how much I learn about the world or how temporarily confused I become, I always return to this understanding: Existence is the creative expansion of unconditional love.

While in various states of unconsciousness, our highest selves are creating realities for us to explore like avatars. As we become more conscious, we merge with these aspects of us and begin to create consciously. We start to use the creative life force that God is to design reality for ourselves. We enter the field of pure potential.

Potential is the energy field of all that could possibly be, held in an empty container called the present moment. It is not a future-oriented concept that defines a set of possible options. Potential only exists in the present, standing before us at all times with a big platter of everything.

Potential is the substance with which you bring dreams to life. It is the inspiration, paint, canvas, brush, and stroke with which you create the picture of your life. As we move from unconsciousness to consciousness, as we awaken from the long slumber, we begin to dream in daylight.

Daylight dreaming should be as routine as morning coffee, weekend napping, and texts to best friends. Your dreams and desires are memos to the divine who waits, feathered quill in hand, to make a to-do list just for you. In states of great awakeness, we quite naturally create only what is good and loving for ourselves and for all.

Dreaming is one of your many superpowers if you can focus on the *whats* and leave the *hows* to quantum physics and the mysterious ways of the all-powerful creator, the one with the fancy pen.

I am dreaming of

> technologies that effortlessly cleanse the planet's waters, winds, recesses and surfaces;

> a biosphere so abundant and diverse there is only ever discovery and delight;

magical music, like a chorus of crickets,
that renews bodies, minds, and spirits;

making friends with dragons and lions,
hummingbirds and lizards;

connecting utterly to what is rare, rooted,
and hallowed in the people I meet;

knowing myself as hallowed too and
seeing what unfolds as a result;

dreaming a dream much bigger than my
groggy mind can conjure.

There's no time like the present could not be a
more apt expression when it comes to inten-
tional dreaming. What do we have to lose?
Our dreams certainly do not come to life from
not dreaming them into existence. Let us see
what we can do.

Dear Human,
Let life love you back.

Life is lived on levels—physical, mental, emotional, and spiritual. You can lose yourself in any one of them and forget all else. When you exist in broad strokes, according to large principles, as part of a mass of humanity, it is easy to forget the ceaseless nuance.

Sweetness, however, like God, is in the details.

What I love most about living in the Midwest is that the weather provides a continuous display of sweet moments. As I write on a nearly June morning at my home in the woods, I am watching the sun play off the broad leaves of a houseplant. It is an astonishing show of light, greenery, and wood. Down the hill, the lake is calm despite the torrential rains we had last night, and the traffic on the highway a mile away is uncommonly quiet. Besides my breath, there is only birdsong, and it is about to break open my heart.

Sweetness does not demand any particular setting. It is revealed in the heavy moment as well as the light, but it is always contained within a moment. And the moment is a portal through which you are transported from the mundane or easily overlooked to the personally profound—if you care to go there.

Sweetness is found in the moment you reach for and find your favorite coffee mug. Or in clean pajamas after a hard day. Or cool water against a weary face.

I cannot contain my foolish enthusiasm for a stubborn patch of lichen peeking through the melting ice, the smell of Palo Santo or a soft rug underfoot. And, oh, the unexpected joy of finding a hair tie in the moment I need it most.

Sweetness cannot be planned for. You cannot go looking for it, nor do you need to. But you may want to prepare a welcoming place by softening the mind, the belly, and the ardent gaze. In fact, round off all the hard edges and sweetness surely will rush in like water into a sandcastle's moat at high tide. Your life, no matter how hard, cruel, or absurd, wants to drown you in gifts of sweetness. When you decide to accept them, you become a vessel for the expression of sweetness. Your thoughts sweeten, your gestures sweeten, your words and actions sweeten until it becomes nearly impossible to hear harshness or taste bitterness. Even the savagery within can be touched by the compassionate weight of your innocent, still-unfolding sweetness.

Sweetness is both small and overriding. Sweetness savored can charge the particles in the cosmos in transcendental ways. It is a real-life filter that renders everything a little more alive, pearlescent, and redeemable. It does not matter who you are or are not, what you have done or have not done, or what you think you deserve or do not. Sweetness is the universe's gift to give, and it does so with reckless abandon. Little tokens, dropped into your pocket, to let you know you are loved.

When I was young, love showed up as thunderbolts and heartbreak. It would come crashing in, sudden and hazardous, and then seem to tiptoe out backward so that I did not notice it going. Where was the charming in-between?

Later, I operated on the notion that love was an emotion, like fury, externally activated. If I felt love, it was because I was convinced I was being loved by him or her or them or that. And when they took their love and left, I was bereft. Loveless.

But whether through wisdom or stubbornness, I have come to see and feel love as something elemental and almost operational. Love is not an emotion. It does not come and go the way happy and sad do. It is both more ordinary and more primordial than I knew.

Love is the energy infusing all things from the wonderful to the miserable, from the sublime to the unbearable. It is us at our best and us at our worst. That is just a cold, hard fact, and love is the absence of judgment about it.

When you love a child, you do not love them only when they are trying their best, being good, and doing things well. You love them when they are writhing on the floor in a tantrum of frustration and confusion. You love them when they refuse, out of rebellion or doubt, to rise to their potential. You love them when they do not realize the impact of their actions on others, or, out of pain, don't care. Sometimes, when they are just being awful, you love them even more because you know they have temporarily forgotten how loved they are. You love them because you know that what they do is not who they are.

You are a child of God. And that is how you are loved. That is how everyone is loved, even the people you feel you must hate or there will be no justice in the world.

It is not easy to accept that nothing exists outside of God's love. It does not seem fair. But sometimes our reluctance to swallow the fact that horrible people and wretched things are loved unconditionally is really about our inability to accept that we, in our horrible wretchedness, are loved unconditionally. But we are. It may be even harder to accept that we wanted to experience everything that we have experienced. But we did. And still, we are loved unconditionally.

If you can love yourself despite these realizations, you have begun to know one of many strange, uncomfortable, and beautiful truths.

Being human should feel like going to camp. Maybe it is a little scary at first because you don't know anyone and you are leaving your parents for the first time. But then you realize everybody is in the same boat. By the end of day one, you know where everything is and how it all works. You feel a wild independence, with some loose supervision, just in case. And then:

You make new friends

Eat meals at the bell and help clear the table

Make arts and crafts, play games,
and build forts

Try things you've never tried before

Lie in the warm sun and dip in the cold lake

Share your sunscreen and bug spray

Sing songs and tell stories after dark

Wake up when the sun rises

Make your bed

Sweep the cabin

See what new adventures await the day

But instead, you might feel like you have dumped your canoe, you are treading deep water, and everyone has gone to lunch without you. And the worst counselors keep throwing you floats on ropes too short to reach you or shame you into swimming for an unreachable shore.

What choice do you have but to cling to illusory promises like your life depended on them?

Letting go and trusting your skills at this point might seem like lunacy because you have been persuaded that you cannot make it on your own.

But you can.

Within you is the strength to release yourself from the powerlessness of false promises. You can reach deep to find the inner resources that not only will save you but bring you to your rightful position as camp MVP, the true and sovereign you.

When you let go, you do not sink. You float.

Because you can, you already are creating the things you desire for yourself and your camp-mates near and far—standards and systems that value and support all life forms without exception, honor love as the guiding principle, encourage personal expression and collabora-tion, and promote robust physical, emotional, and spiritual well-being. It is the desire itself that has set this new world into motion. As the new is sewn piece by piece from the quantum fabric, the old becomes obsolete and falls away.

This is the moment in which we find ourselves—smack dab between the falling away and the creation of the new. It may feel chaotic, but it is divine order in irreversible flow.

Heaven on Earth is your inevitable inheritance. It is not something you have to fight to create or wrestle from the hands of another. Tech-nically, it already exists because everything already exists, accessed through the portal of your magical heart. There, you are free to live without fear, dream your dreams, explore your gifts, and have fun with your people.

Just like camp.

In 2017 I traveled to Tunisia with a group of fellow seekers. There, between the Atlas Mountains and the Mediterranean Sea, I experienced many unfolding miracles but none so deeply moving as the Islamic call to prayer. I understood the call to prayer to be a call to presence—a constant asking to observe the sacred in our everyday lives. The call permeates all of life and never skips a day because we tend to need continuous reminder. I desperately wanted the call to be part of my life, but I reside in the Midwest, not the Middle East.

Since then, the only thing I have found that can bring me close to that kind of reverence for the present is the awareness of my breath. Now, I have a practice as present as the call to prayer, and it has become my highest and holiest devotion. I breathe.

At night before I sleep and first thing upon waking, I place my hands over my heart and let my entire body be filled with the breath of life. It is a prayer of hope—please breathe me while I sleep. It is a prayer of thanks at first light. It is a gathering of the distance between night and day, fears and dreams, lost and found.

But it was not always so. Years ago, we decided to build a new home for our family. This one decision, which I simultaneously dreaded and embraced, became the catalyst for many tectonic shifts.

We moved into a temporary rental on the other side of town with our four kids and big dog. Nearly every morning and afternoon for the next 18 months, I would drive my children to and from their four different schools. In addition to all of the regular duties of motherhood—the nonstop love and attention, schedules, homework, sports, activities, appointments, friends, shopping, cooking, laundry, cleaning, birthdays, holidays, outings, projects—I now also was overseeing the budget, design, and construction of our new home. Many things got mangled in the process. By the time we moved in, I was a bundle of frayed nerves and dashed hopes.

Everything piled up, layer after claustrophobic layer, as stress moved into unwellness then veered into crisis. I barely slept. I was too terrified to cry. I was self-shamed into silence for being so miserable in such a beautiful and privileged life. Knowing my situation was not some random fate but rather a matter of choice made it all the more difficult to admit I was drowning.

In my life at that time, everything was output. Nothing was coming in—no time for stillness, no self-nurturing, no peaceful resets. My gratitude had become tinged with desperation, like, *Please, God, don't punish me for being so blessed*. My mind spinning, I was barely breathing.

My life was breaking down. Or more accurately, my life was breaking me down. And I let it. Slowly, over time, I began to breathe again. As my breath deepened, I started to appreciate that breathing is not just a mechanical partnership between the brain and lungs, just as art is not solely a matter of hands and brushes.

In yoga, it is said that prana, the life force energy, rides on the breath. This image reminds me of the tale of Arjuna, the warrior human, and Krishna, his divine chariot driver, from The Bhagavad Gita. In both examples, the mundane is married to the transcendent.

Now, when things are really difficult or really good, I climb into the lap of my cosmic mother, rest my head in the crook of her arm, and allow our lungs to rise and fall in sync. Sometimes I envision the breath as light, and then my cells become flooded with an illuminated love that absolves all trouble. On occasion, I know that when I breathe in, the universe contracts ever so slightly. And when I breathe out, it expands exponentially. My lungs become it, and it becomes me.

My inability to be present in my overwhelming life corresponded directly to my inability to breathe fully. The tension and stress of life promoted shallow breathing, which amplified the anxiety and depression. Devoting myself to breathing deeply and consciously has helped me through everything that has ever threatened my peace—from mental tirades, loss of love and loved ones, physical challenges, and uncorralled fear.

I still sometimes fall into the unconsciousness of allowing my breath to grow shallow, but not for long. Now, I understand that we are never forced into communion with the miraculous. The invitation stands. And we accept it with every breath.

I'm alone here
Dizzy and lost
Spinning through space
With a planet attached to my feet
I'm clinging to the outer tip
Of the windmill's blade
Bent on swinging me loose
When sometimes I feel your breath
Breathing inside of mine
I move to the center of everything
And stand in the storm's mild eye

A teacher I follow on social media once said that gratitude is the highest currency. This idea took root in me. If there is a better way to pay respect than to express your deepest gratitude, I have not found it.

An awake person knows this and spends their days never forgetting to thank everyone and everything. But what you may not see, unless you are really wide awake, is how all of life is expressing its gratitude for *you*.

We are living components of a dynamic system that is fueled by reciprocity. Scientists have proven that crops respond more favorably to mindful, moderate harvesting than either being left untouched or overharvested. There is no greed or wanting in the exchange of oxygen and carbon dioxide between humans and trees. It occurs in perfect balance, without negotiation. In my book, it is not a stretch to imagine that the natural world is as grateful for you as you are for it. I know this when I am sitting at the seaside watching the sun glimmer through the water, feeling a love so large it cannot possibly be wholly self-generated.

Imagine what a day would be like if you could accept that the birds are singing just for you, or that the Earth longs for your bare footsteps each day. What would it feel like to know that the wind serves to wash you free and clear of lesser energies or that the campfire drew strength from your outstretched hands? Could you then understand that the treasures you bring into your house to make it a home are honored to bring you kinship and comfort?

Gratitude of this magnitude calls for a soft-hearted yielding to the suspicion that *every-thing* is conspiring in your favor. To always be the expresser of gratitude, and never to receive it, is to miss the point entirely. Gratitude is the natural response to being loved. If you are grateful for something, it is because it is loving you.

Life itself looks for you in every cafe, on every street corner, and through the eyes of every potential friend, hoping for a meaningful chance encounter. The world you create with your curating gaze, creates itself to lay down gifts of gratitude before you.

What you are grateful for, is grateful for you.

Dear Human,
You are a little ho-hum and
profoundly marvelous.

have heard a thousand times that we are sur-
rounded by unseen beings of light who are
cheering us on, acknowledging that incarnat-
ing as a human on planet Earth at this time is
one of the most difficult assignments and rarest
privileges in the omniverse. When I need to
feel comforted, I find this comforting.

I know many people who have varying degrees
of insight about their experiences as other life
forms in other lifetimes in other dimensions.
This makes sense because, apparently, we are
everywhere all at once.

One morning, my daughter came down for
breakfast and wearily announced that she was
starting a GoFundMe campaign to send her
back to her home planet. It was then I realized
she was only on loan to me. And from the time
one of my sons was an infant, he seemed to
be working through struggles that played out
in his dreams and periodically turned him
melancholy for no reason. It was then I knew
he had lived before.

By comparison, my own experience has been rather ordinary. When I look in the mirror each morning I see the person I have been and the one I have become. But if I am being honest, in my mind's eye, I see a council of elders standing in a circle above my head, not all of them human. And recently, for a long moment, I experienced myself solely as a tone, like a celestial song with just one pure and all-encompassing note. Nearly every day now, I encounter some new thing that leaves me scratching my head and sometimes pulling the wool over my own eyes.

In this strange world, things are not outlandish to me. Perhaps because I have been primed by seeing (yes, okay, mostly sleeping through) all of the *Star Trek* and *Star Wars* movies. Frankly, I have been presented with less believable scenarios.

But what stirs me more than any of it and perhaps most in this world is a visit to Apple Valley Natural Foods, a half-hour's drive from my home, which I discovered en route to a new hiking trail. It is the kind of small-town grocery store where bright yellow posters with bold black lettering advertise 29-cent apples and deep discounts on Bisquick.

Inside, the store is divided into two sections. To the left, marked by patchy linoleum and too-dim lighting, all the basic brands sit side-by-side with a wide variety of off-brand, ethnic and old-timey items. Behind the deli case, there are big tubes of processed meats as well as deviled duck eggs, things floating in murky pickling liquid, and marshmallowed Jell-O rings. On one visit this summer, I saw a mound of something pink in a ceramic dish labeled *Guess What Salad*. I appreciated the intrigue, but took a pass on it nonetheless.

This bit of Apple Valley real estate is where, I imagine, old farmers' wives come to find the secret ingredients featured in their grandmothers' recipes. Items destined, and perhaps deservedly so, to become extinct.

The population here is diverse, so it is common to see people in traditional dress. The small college nearby supplies a steady flow of budget-minded students. You can see just by looking that folks around here work long hours and try to enjoy simple pleasures when life permits. On any given day, you will not mistake this heartland place for anyplace coastal, if you know what I mean.

On the far side of Produce, you will find rows of high-end, small-batch items like those that line the shelves at upscale grocery stores. There is a large assortment of healthy foods plus supplements, vitamins, compounds, extracts, tinctures, oils, and blends, representing ancient and modern ideas about wellness. I make the drive to get organic this and non-GMO that, and there are others here doing the same, I suspect.

Curiously wedged between the fancy food and the sea of bottles, bins, and pots, like an alternate universe, is a double-sided aisle stuffed full of commune-size canned vegetarian meats and other food-like products. I have never seen a soul in this aisle except for me, and my *Cults Near Me* internet search turned up absolutely nothing.

Mysteries aside, Apple Valley is a strange and special place. Set inside a nondescript strip mall in a little town in rural Michigan, it is both the most unusual and thoroughly typical grocery store I have ever stepped foot in. If you are dashing in for a few things, you might miss it. If you do not care to see what is happening in there, you won't. But if you meander, take some time to observe, you might catch a glimpse of something unexpected, rare, and beautiful—a microcosm of the human collective. Right here at the Apple Valley.

I love this little store with its weirdly curated spaces and shoppers of every variety so much it hurts. When I shop, I take my time, gazing admiringly at our diversity. I try to keep my enthusiasm in check as best I can so I don't arouse suspicion or alarm. No one else seems to notice the treasure in our midst.

Sometimes I stay longer hoping to strike up a conversation. Often I buy extra to make sure it stays open. I wonder if Apply Valley is the only place in the universe that truly is for everyone.

I feel close to tears each time I consider how slightly ho-hum and profoundly marvelous this really is. Just like life itself. Think about it—there are nearly eight billion different ways of being in the world. Each of us has differing characteristics, circumstances, and views on life. We have been through things that have shattered us and other things that have made us whole again, and we never know from one day to the next which of these two we will experience. We lie down at night with our troubles and wake up each morning with hope. And all any of us wants is to feed ourselves something familiar. To care for our loved ones and to be nourished by love. To put a few things in our basket so we can have a little something nice for lunch.

I would never claim to know all that is occurring here on Earth and beyond. I know we each have reasons for being here that are both collective and personal. And, above all, sacred. I know there are special things we each bring to the table and lessons we each came to learn. And yet, to be human is not that rare. You can find one on every street corner.

We sometimes forget that it has taken a confluence of a million miracles to create each of us into being. We are quite literally galaxies of energized particles, with more space than matter, held together by an invisible force, exhibiting independent will, interacting according to some unknowable order. We think, we feel, we taste, and we touch. We sing, dance, play, create, change, and love.

Can you fathom the scope of it—each one of us representing untold phenomenon continuously colliding, shifting, and evolving in some sort of spectacular symphonic masterpiece? I can't.

But I feel it every time I visit Apple Valley.

We sometimes forget that the craziness of our times and the burdens of our struggles are small potatoes compared to our power and purpose. One smile of understanding at a frazzled mom with a cranky toddler obliterates worlds of shadow. One generous tip for a tired server cures a thousand slights. One extra-long embrace for a grieving friend shakes the cobwebs off our collective despair.

We are not reaching for divine potential; we are the infinite articulation of divine expression.

We are born as stars, destined to become suns, ordained to become universes. As we step into the mystical phosphorescence of endless life, the field of limitlessness itself expands in a paradoxical puzzle that wants to break my brain and solve my heart. And still, this seems both too small and not simple enough.

We are the pure prism through which God gazes at the kaleidoscopic lavishness of its own creation. Amid an endless sea of curiosities and wonder, we are all the miracles ever set loose in the cosmos.

We are human—a little ho-hum and profoundly marvelous.

And, there is no end.

ACKNOWLEDGMENTS

My life is stocked to the gills with angels of Earth who arrive unbeckoned with love and support, who remain present and accepting as I stumble and soar on my chosen path. I hope you each feel as lifted as I do by our life collaboration—the holy growth, discovery, astonishment, and laughter. I pray you each are blessed a thousandfold. I love you so much more than words can convey.

Jude Roche, Alexa Schill, Diana Schieke, Lisa Marie Trunkenbolz, Sheri Bagwell, Tera Abelson, Meggan Riley, Katie Garten Briscoe, Lisa Stokke, Ashley Livingston, Nancy Petrone, Thea Sullivan, Krysta Baugh, Sejal Acharya, Jan Courter, Andrea Reiners, Gretchen Eck, Nancy Eck, Al Eck, Shirley Eck, Christina Farrell, Ben Rinnenbach, Jason Garrett, Aaron Ogden, Matthew Patti, Sarah Holehouse, Jennifer Falchi, Julie Mackey, Lonnie Packard, Linda

Anderson, Christine Howard, Taylor Godfrey, Elle Windsong, and Zon Carvalho.

I am especially grateful for the friendship, enthusiasm, and talents of Alexandrea Blackham.

Thank you, too, to Joie Scott at Sunset 6, Niki Rhoads at Colourline, the dream teams at Luminare Press and Kava Diem Coffee, the lovers of Bloom Yoga, all the brave guests of the Alive & Kicking podcast, and the many teachers who do not know my name but have carried me on their wave of generosity.

To my beloved Lake Michigan and the wooded wonderlands at her shore, I send gratitude for your endless revelation and support.

Finally, it may seem as though without Andy, Wes, Evan, and Audrey Eck, I might never have learned a thing in this world, and I suspect this might be true. With the greatest love I have ever known, thank you.

CPSIA information can be obtained
at www.ICGtesting.com
Printed in the USA
LVHW082040260721
693767LV00002B/4/J

9 781736 583128